At Your Service

NEIL DIXON

At Your Service

A COMMENTARY ON
The Methodist Service Book

WIPF & STOCK · Eugene, Oregon

Wipf and Stock Publishers
199 W 8th Ave, Suite 3
Eugene, OR 97401

At Your Service
A Commentary on The Methodist Service Book
By Dixon, Neil
Copyright©1976 Methodist Publishing - Epworth Press
ISBN 13: 978-1-5326-3076-7
Publication date 4/7/2017
Previously published by Epworth Press, 1976

Every effort has been made to trace the current copyright
owner of this publication but without success. If you have
any information or interest in the copyright, please contact the publishers.

Contents

	Preface	7
	Some Words	9
1	Introduction	11
2	The Sunday Service (1)	20
3	The Sunday Service (2)	28
4	The Sunday Service (3)	36
5	The Baptism of Infants	46
6	Confirmation	53
7	The Covenant Service	62
8	The Marriage Service	70
9	The Burial or Cremation of the Dead	78
10	The Ordination of Ministers	85
	Addendum	94

Preface

The publication of *The Methodist Service Book* is an important landmark in the story of Methodist worship, and when I was invited to write a Cell Book about it, I was conscious both that the invitation was an honour and that it carried with it a heavy responsibility. It has been my aim to try to do justice to the contents of the new Service Book; but I realized from the outset that my aim was unattainable.

The new services obviously invite comparison with the contents of *The Book of Offices* (1936), and to some extent I have made such comparisons. In the main, however, I have tended to write about the new services in their own right, setting them in the context of contemporary worship and the theology which they express. It should go without saying that individual readers and groups using this book as a basis for discussion will need to refer frequently to copies of *The Methodist Service Book*.

One chapter is devoted to each service in *The Methodist Service Book*, with two exceptions. THE SUNDAY SERVICE is so important, both as an order for the celebration of the Lord's Supper and as an outline for other services, that I have spread my comments on it over three chapters, after the introduction. On the other hand, THE ORDER OF SERVICE FOR THE ADMINISTRATION OF THE LORD'S SUPPER which is reproduced from the *The Book of Offices* is so familiar to Methodists and so much has been written about it, that less comment seemed to be required here. Accordingly only part of a chapter is about that service, though this fact is not to be taken as an indication of my opinion of the service.

Copious footnotes could have been supplied; but they would have made the book too long and most readers would probably not have welcomed them. Footnotes have therefore been kept to a minimum; and where they occur, they almost invariably refer to books which should be readily accessible to readers—most ministers and local preachers will have copies.

Worship is the centre of the corporate life of the Church, and because it is so vital it must constantly be renewed. *The Methodist Service Book* is a successful attempt to provide worthy acts of worship for today's Church, and thereby to help local churches to renew their liturgical life. I hope that this short introduction to the Service Book may make a modest contribution towards the same end.

August 1975   NEIL DIXON

Some Words

As far as possible, technical terms used by expert liturgists have been avoided in these pages, but a few words call for explanation:

LITURGY: This word is sometimes used rather loosely to distinguish formal acts of worship (which are called 'liturgical') from free services. Thus a man might say that he likes 'liturgical' services, meaning that he approves of acts of worship governed by a service book. Strictly speaking, however, the words 'liturgy' and 'worship' can be interchanged. 'Liturgy' is derived from two Greek words and literally means 'the work of the people': liturgy is the supreme service rendered to God by his people. In this book we use 'liturgy' in this strict sense, meaning simply 'worship'; hence 'a liturgy' means a form of service, 'liturgical' means 'pertaining to worship', and 'a liturgist' is a writer or compiler of liturgies.

THE EUCHARIST: The Sacrament of the Lord's Supper has been known by many names, one of which, 'Eucharist', is now widely used in many denominations. Derived from a Greek word meaning 'thanksgiving', the term reflects the idea of celebration which is central to this sacrament. So far 'Eucharist' has not been in common use in Methodism and is not, indeed, to be found in *The Methodist Service Book*, but the word is so useful as a succinct title that it has been used in a number of places in this book.

CONFIRMATION: Literally, 'strengthening'. This word has come to be used in Methodism recently, not simply because other denominations use it, but because it aptly describes the service of reception into full membership, in which the Church asks the Holy Spirit to confirm as disciples of Jesus those who have previously been baptized. Confirmation is the second part of entry into the Church, Baptism being the first.

RITE: A form of service, a liturgy.

RUBRIC: All formal acts of worship include rubrics, which are instructions for minister and congregation (e.g. 'All stand'). Originally, rubrics were so-called because they were printed in red; this practice has been adopted in *The Methodist Service Book*.

ORDINANCE: An authorized form of service.

1 Introduction

Some churches, notably the Roman Catholic Church and the Church of England, almost invariably use in their worship formal services prescribed in prayer books. Other denominations, including most Free Churches, have traditionally had little use for set services and have emphasized the value of 'free' worship. The Methodist Church, however, in its worship as in other respects, cannot be classified so easily; on the whole it has avoided both extremes by making use of both formal and free worship.

Thus John Wesley, Anglican priest and founder of Methodism, effusively praised *The Book of Common Prayer* (1662) and commended it to his followers; but he did not hesitate to conduct free services or to pray extempore. The dual tradition has survived to this day. The majority of Methodist services, it is true, are in theory 'free'—though often their structure and content have become fossilized; they are not, in a strict sense, formal, and they do not require the use of a service book. At the same time, for the sacraments of Baptism and the Lord's Supper and for occasional services such as Reception into Full Membership, the Covenant Service, Marriage, Burial, and Ordination, Methodists have had a succession of service books that can trace their ancestry to Wesley, and beyond him to *The Book of Common Prayer*. The immediate predecessor of *The Methodist Service*

Book was *The Book of Offices* (1936); for nearly forty years the majority of Methodist churches have made use of it. Why is a new book needed?

The Preface to *The Methodist Service Book* provides some answers to this question, which will no doubt be asked in many churches. First, we are reminded of the developments that have occurred since 1936 in the study of worship. The Liturgical Movement[1] has emphasized important aspects of worship which *The Book of Offices* does not adequately express. By studying the origins of Christian worship, the Movement has also made available new insights into the question of how worship should be structured. In order to take account of these emphases and discoveries, a new service book was needed.

Other churches have felt the same need. Working independently, but frequently consulting one another, the major denominations in Britain have, for ten years or so, been hard at work in producing new forms of worship. During this period, for example, the Roman Catholics have revised the Mass and other services and translated them into English; and the Church of England has issued various experimental services, one of which, a eucharistic rite popularly known as 'Series 3', is now widely used. Like Methodism, these denominations and others have felt the impact of the Liturgical Movement and responded to its influence.

---

[1] For a summary of the emphases of the Liturgical Movement, see Neil Dixon, *Approach with Joy*, Epworth Press, 1975, pp. 47 f.

INTRODUCTION

Another important factor which has led Methodism and other churches to draw up new forms of service is the change that has taken place in recent years in the language of worship. Quite spontaneously, many preachers have started to express themselves in a style which is simpler and more direct than that which was in vogue forty years ago. The language of *The Book of Offices* is, by and large, much more than forty years old; a good deal of it has survived unchanged from the period of Elizabeth I. There is no doubt that this language is often extremely beautiful. But what about clarity and intelligibility? The majority of modern worshippers are obliged, when they turn to *The Book of Offices*, to use thought forms and language which are quite foreign to their normal experience. Excellent new translations of the Bible have clearly shown that the Scriptures can best come alive for a man if they are expressed in his own language and not in that of his distant forebears. The same argument applies to the rest of worship.

For these reasons, the Methodist Conference has now authorized *The Methodist Service Book*. This authorization follows about ten years of work. During the 1960s the Faith and Order Committee drafted forms of service which were issued, with the authority of the Conference, for experimental use. Comments and criticisms were invited from rank and file worshippers, from Methodist churches overseas, and from scholars of other denominations. In the light of these consultations, the services were revised and the final drafts were approved by the Conferences of 1974 and 1975.

The Order of Service for the Administration of the Lord's Supper

With one exception, all the services included in *The Methodist Service Book* are new. The exception is THE ORDER OF SERVICE FOR THE ADMINISTRATION OF THE LORD'S SUPPER, which was included in *The Book of Offices* and is reproduced here with revised rubrics. This service is in fact an amended version of the eucharistic rite of *The Book of Common Prayer* (1662). It has been included in *The Methodist Service Book* because of its intrinsic merit, the high regard in which it is widely held, and its familiarity.

The service begins with the Lord's Prayer and the Collect for Purity ('Almighty God, unto whom all hearts be open...'), both said by the minister alone. This is a quaint survival of a medieval practice; the priest used to say prayers of his own as a personal act of preparation before the service proper began. Then either the Commandments of the Lord Jesus or the Ten Commandments are read, the congregation making suitable responses. This is intended to encourage worshippers towards penitence—a strong emphasis upon confession and forgiveness is a notable characteristic of this rite.

Next follow the Collect of the Day, the Epistle and the Gospel. Both collects and Bible readings are discussed more fully in Chapters Two and Four, and need not be considered here, except to remark that it has been the wisdom of the Church to recognize, from the earliest days, that the reading of Scripture and the celebration of the Lord's Supper belong together intimately. The position of the sermon and the Nicene

INTRODUCTION

Creed may be varied; either may precede the other. (Oddly enough, no fixed place was allotted to the sermon in 1936, though the introductory rubrics envisaged that one would normally be preached. This has been remedied in the new rubrics.) The Nicene Creed has long been associated with the Eucharist, and as a summary of the Church's faith, it is appropriate that it should be recited after either the readings or the sermon.

After an offering for the poor has been collected during the reading of Scripture sentences, the minister leads the congregation in the Prayer for the Church Militant. This is a long prayer and it has been criticized for being too domestic in its concerns: apart from a section about kings, princes and governors (who are required to be Christians) and a reference to the sick and those in trouble, it is wholly concerned with the internal life of the Church. Intercession (prayer for others) should ideally be much wider in scope.

Words of Invitation follow, exhorting the congregation to examine their hearts and consciences, referring to the institution of the sacrament by Jesus, and inviting the congregation to 'draw near with faith'. The minister and congregation say a prayer of confession (though hardly ever meekly kneeling upon their knees, and probably never with the congregation repeating the words after the minister, both of which practices are enjoined upon them). The minister says a diluted form of absolution (a declaration of God's forgiveness), the strength of which is diminished by the substitution of 'us' for the traditional 'you'. The

'Confortable Words' lead into the *Sursum* Corda ('Lift up your hearts'). This is one of the few points in this rite where there is any emphasis upon joy. Before the congregation joins in the *Sanctus* ('Holy, Holy, Holy'), a Proper Preface is said on certain festival days. Such prefaces have gone out of fashion in some liturgical circles; they are not encouraged in THE SUNDAY SERVICE (though 'Series 3' retains them) on the grounds that the whole Gospel, not just part of it, can and should be celebrated in every eucharistic service.

The Prayer of Humble Access ('We do not presume...'), now said by the minister, has been a feature of Anglican eucharistic rites and their derivatives since 1549. It is a beautiful prayer, held in high regard by many people, but it may be wondered whether we really ought to be stressing our unworthiness and sinfulness at this point in the service. The Prayer of Humble Access is indeed consistent with the general mood of this rite; but, as we shall see, it does not fit so neatly into THE SUNDAY SERVICE.

The Prayer of Consecration which follows includes the Words of Institution (the account of what Jesus said and did at the Last Supper). After the people have received the bread and the wine and have prayed silently, the Lord's Prayer is said by all, followed by one of two prayers of self-offering and thanksgiving and the ancient hymn 'Glory be to God on High' (*Gloria in Excelsis*). This hymn, newly translated, is also included in THE SUNDAY SERVICE, but in a better position—near the beginning of the rite, where its twin

INTRODUCTION

notes of penitence and praise are more appropriately sounded. The minister then dismisses the congregation with two blessings.

As an amended form of a rite which is substantially over four hundred years old, the 1936 service has undoubtedly stood the test of time. That it still means so much to so many people is itself a tribute to those who originally compiled it and those who have since revised it. Its words have become rich in association; its balanced sentences flow superbly; its form and content are part of the Methodist heritage and will long remain so.

But it is well known that old age inevitably produces weaknesses of one sort or another; and this service, beloved as it is, has increasingly been found inadequate in the following ways:

1. Its language is archaic. As we have previously said, the ideal language of worship is the normal language of the worshipper, not that of a long-departed age. It may be thought that the familiarity of this service and the fact that there are very few really obscure passages in it compensate for its archaic character. Yet it is often very wordy (see, for example, the Prayer for the Church Militant), and to those who have not been accustomed to its use from infancy, its language and indeed its thought-forms seem remote from normal experience.

2. Perhaps more seriously, it is theologically defective. One notable discovery of the Liturgical Movement is that celebration is a key concept in worship. Joy and thanksgiving should set the tone of services;

self-examination and penitence, while having a place, should not predominate. But in this rite:

(a) There is a very strong emphasis on penitence. At the beginning of the service, the Commandments invoke repentance; there is a long exhortation to self-examination, followed by a prayer of confession in the middle of the service; the Prayer of Humble Access and the Prayer of Consecration are both full of references to sin; the first post-communion prayer and even 'Glory be to God on High' reflect this obsession.

(b) There is frequent reference to the Cross, but little to the Resurrection. It is an important liturgical principle that 'every Sunday is a little Easter' —on the day on which Jesus was raised from the dead, his people gather to celebrate his Resurrection. This rite does not give expression to that principle.

(c) At the heart of a eucharistic service, we should expect to find a prayer of thanksgiving, reflecting the action of Jesus ('he gave thanks') at the Last Supper. Instead, just before communion, we find a prayer of consecration, from which the note of thanksgiving is conspicuously absent. This is a most serious defect.

For reasons such as these, an alternative form of eucharistic service has been considered necessary and has been provided in THE SUNDAY SERVICE. But so much esteem for the 1936 service still exists, that THE SUNDAY SERVICE will not absolutely supersede it; nor is that the intention of the Conference. The old service

INTRODUCTION

is still available in *The Methodist Service Book*, alongside the new services, for the use of those who value it.

Questions for discussion
1. Discuss your feelings for and against the publication of *The Methodist Service Book*. Are the arguments for superseding *The Book of Offices* strong enough?

2. Compare the language and concerns of the Prayer for the Church in *The Book of Offices* with the Intercessions (pp. B7–B9) in THE SUNDAY SERVICE.

3. Discuss the merits and demerits of the 1936 Communion Service.

4. Discuss the advantages and disadvantages of both formal and free services.

2 The Sunday Service (1)

THE SUNDAY SERVICE takes its title from the first service book published by John Wesley, *The Sunday Service of the Methodists in North America, with other occasional Services*. The new service provides for full celebrations of the Lord's Supper—into which other rites, such as Baptism and Confirmation, can be inserted when appropriate—and also supplies material for use when there is no Communion.

There can be no doubt that the Sacrament of the Lord's Supper occupied the central place in the worship of the Early Church, and in many Christian churches, this sacrament is still celebrated each week as the principal act of worship. A high regard for the Eucharist is one part of the Methodist heritage that has unfortunately been lost. John Wesley himself received the bread and the wine at least once each week—and often twice—throughout his adult life. In the nineteenth century, great emphasis was placed on sermons; around the same time, Methodists reacted strongly against the 'High Church' tendencies of the Oxford Movement in the Church of England which laid great stress upon the sacraments; and both these factors led to a regrettable undervaluation of the Lord's Supper among Methodists. So, until quite recently, it has been the widespread custom to append a drastically abridged form of the Communion Service to a full-length preaching service

THE SUNDAY SERVICE (1)

once a month or even less frequently. Many people, it is true, were becoming dissatisfied with this practice, and some churches began to use one of the two Communion Services from *The Book of Offices* in full (as other churches had long been doing); but one suspects that the publication in 1968 of the experimental form of THE SUNDAY SERVICE had the greatest impact in causing many ministers and congregations to review their practice.

The Lord's Supper is not an optional extra. It is the central act of Christian worship. It is not fitting that a few special prayers and actions should be added on to a lengthy and unrelated preaching service; the act of receiving bread and wine should rather be the culmination of a complete and coherent act of worship. Two full services were provided in 1936; they were almost always used in abridged forms. It seems probable, and is greatly to be hoped, that THE SUNDAY SERVICE will be used in full, and used frequently.

When there is to be a celebration of the Lord's Supper, THE SUNDAY SERVICE falls into three parts:

The Preparation
The Ministry of the Word
The Lord's Supper.

1. The Preparation

Seven items are listed in this section of the service, but only one of these, the Collect of the Day, is marked with the symbol used in this rite to indicate the basic elements which should not be omitted. The

Collect for Purity has been used for centuries as part of the Preparation, and it is an excellent prayer of invocation. The version printed here is a neat 'You' version of the original. God is addressed as 'You' throughout the new services, a development which is to be welcomed. It is sometimes said that 'Thou' is a mode of expression which emphasizes the 'otherness' and majesty of God; but it is too archaic a term for the living God, too remote for the one whom Jesus taught us to call 'Father'. 'You' has been gaining ground over 'Thou' for some years; and although the older form of address will linger on in many places for years to come, the seal of approval for the new style has been clearly applied in *The Methodist Service Book*.

The General Directions indicate the times when the Commandments may most appropriately be used. The prayer of confession (borrowed from 'Series 3') should be used on most occasions, for it is right that our approach to God should include penitence; but at great festivals such as Easter, when the mood of worshippers should be specially joyful, the confession can be omitted. Whenever it is said, it should be followed by the declaration of forgiveness: the scriptural assurance that the sin we have confessed is forgiven is an important part of worship and makes us bold to continue with our worship with joyful and peaceful hearts.

The Collect of the Day may either precede or follow the second hymn (for which 'Glory to God in the highest' may be substituted). Collects are short prayers which gather together—collect—themes appropriate to the occasion. COLLECTS, LESSONS AND PSALMS, which is included in *The Methodist Service Book*, provides a collect for each Sunday of the year and for other special days. The new translation of *Gloria in Excelsis* was produced by the International Consultation on English Texts; since this hymn combines adoration and penitence its use at this point is very appropriate. Some liturgists think that 'Glory to God in the highest' should not be said or sung in every eucharistic service; it is worthy to be reserved for special occasions, such as the great festivals. There are indeed other advantages in singing some other hymn at this point; a hymn may be chosen to link the collect with the Scripture readings which are to follow.

2. The Ministry of the Word

'The worship of the Church is the offering of praise and prayer in which God's Word is read and preached, and in its fullness it includes the Lord's Supper...', state the General Directions in THE SUNDAY SERVICE. The Early Church preserved a balance between Word and Sacrament which later generations of Christians unfortunately lost. Churches have tended either to emphasize the reading and preaching of Scripture to such an extent that the Lord's Supper was undervalued—as has happened in most Free Churches—or to concentrate on the Eucharist at the expense of the preaching (though not necessarily the reading) of the Word; this has been true for many centuries of the Roman Catholic Church. In recent years, under the influence of the Liturgical Movement, most denominations have made an attempt to restore the balance. Thus preaching is coming into its own in churches which have long neglected it, and, as we have previously suggested, the importance of the Eucharist is now more clearly recognized in Methodism and the Free Churches.

Word and Sacrament belong together, and every celebration of the Lord's Supper should include readings from Scripture. THE SUNDAY SERVICE provides for two or three readings: either an Old Testament lesson, or an Epistle, or both; and a Gospel. (The Epistle may be from any New Testament book other than the four Gospels.) If all three lessons are read, the life of Israel, the faith and practice of the Early Church, and the life and teaching of Jesus are all represented. By long tradition, the Gospel is read last; and sentences to precede and follow it are provided in THE SUNDAY SERVICE. 'It is fitting to stand for the Gospel' (General Directions). These observances do not detract from the importance of the other readings, but they do emphasize the special significance of the Gospels as direct witnesses to the deeds and words of our Lord himself.

How are the readings chosen? Some preachers invariably choose Bible readings to fit in with their sermons; ministers who normally do this will probably not change their practice when they use THE SUNDAY SERVICE. But like other churches, Methodism has a lectionary—a scheme which assigns readings to every Sunday and other special days during the year. This lectionary is to be found in COLLECTS, LESSONS AND PSALMS. Its use is to be commended. A glance at the

THE SUNDAY SERVICE (1)

themes which arise out of the selected lessons will show how many aspects of the Christian Faith are covered by the lectionary each year. It is highly unlikely that any arbitrary choice of readings would provide such comprehensive coverage of Scripture in such a logical order.

Objections to the use of the lectionary and answers to those objections can be found elsewhere.[1] Here we are more concerned with the way in which the lectionary should be used, if it is adopted. Apart from psalms, three readings are provided for each Sunday morning and two for each Sunday evening. The morning service is assumed to be the principal act of worship; but if the Lord's Supper is celebrated in the evening, the two tables may be reversed, or the morning lessons of the other year (for the lectionary covers a two-year period) may be read. The 'controlling lesson' is printed in bold type; this is the passage which determines the theme for the day and it should not therefore be omitted. If only two readings are required, one of the other lessons may be left out.

COLLECTS, LESSONS AND PSALMS is based on the proposals of the Joint Liturgical Group, an interdenominational body on which Methodism is represented. Other churches have also accepted the Group's recommendations with minor alterations, with the result that the lectionaries of several denominations in Great Britain are very similar.

After the Gospel, the sermon is preached. Sermons

[1] See *Worship and Preaching*, June 1973, pp. 2 ff; and Neil Dixon, *Approach with Joy*, pp. 36 f.

have come under fire in recent years, sometimes with good reason. Long, rambling homilies, expressing vaguely religious sentiments, and pleasant talks, stringing together amusing stories, have quite rightly been condemned by thinking worshippers. It has also been pointed out that monologues are not very effective means of communication. Everyone knows how easily the mind can wander during sermons, when the least thing can distract us. There may well be other means of communication at least as effective as sermons, and many churches have experienced worship in new styles which makes little or no use of formal preaching. But, at its best, the sermon is not to be despised. It is important that the Word of God should be not only read but expounded and related to the experience of those who have heard it. Sermons need not be lengthy, for there is no virtue in quantity alone; and there is no conceivable reason why they should be dull. A lively exposition of part of the Bible, showing how it is relevant to the lives of the worshippers, is a significant part of a service. In Chapter Four we shall discuss more fully the relationship between sermons and other acts of worship.

Among other things, worship is a two-way conversation. God speaks to us; we speak to God. In the Ministry of the Word, we listen for the voice of God as the Scriptures are read and expounded; then we respond. In THE SUNDAY SERVICE response begins with intercession—prayer for others. This is highly appropriate, for the good news of the Gospel is not for us alone: it is for the whole world, which is God's concern and ours. Apart from the prayer of intercession

THE SUNDAY SERVICE (1)

printed in the service itself, four other forms are supplied as appendices, three of which are borrowed from overseas sources. We pray for world peace, for our own country, for those in special need, and for the world-wide Church. All five prayers of intercession allow for variation and the inclusion of specific topics of concern. The Lord's Prayer follows the intercessions.

The Grace may next be said, and opportunity may be given for people to leave the service. The practice of slipping away before Communion is to be discouraged, for the Lord's Supper is not an optional extra to Christian worship; 'it is the privilege and duty of members of the Methodist Church to avail themselves of this Sacrament' (General Directions, quoting the Deed of Union). But there may, from time to time, be those present who do not wish to stay to the Lord's Supper or children who do not wish to come forward for a blessing; so provision is made for the departure of those who leave.

Questions for discussion

1. Do you agree that '*in its fullness*', 'the worship of the Church . . . includes the Lord's Supper'?

2. Discuss the value of the regular use of the lectionary and the collects.

3. Why is prayer for others a vital part of worship?

4. Compare the new translation of *Glory to God in the highest* with the older and more familiar version. Which do you prefer, and why?

3 The Sunday Service (2)

3. The Lord's Supper

The Lord's Supper proper begins with the Peace. This is a very ancient ceremony, which originates in the Kiss of Peace: 'Greet one another with a holy kiss' (I Thessalonians 5:26). No suggestion is made in THE SUNDAY SERVICE that this particular practice should be restored! The Peace is exchanged verbally, between minister and congregation; it may then be 'given throughout the congregation by a handclasp from one member to another'. There is much to be said in favour of this action, which invites the active participation of every worshipper, and emphasizes the congregation's love and unity in Christ. Some people, however, find it embarrassing.

The Nicene Creed may be said. This creed has long been associated with the Eucharist, but some liturgists feel that, like 'Glory to God in the highest', it is best reserved for special occasions, partly because it covers much the same ground as the great prayer of thanksgiving which follows later. But others feel that, after the reading and preaching of the Word, a summary of the Church's Faith is never out of place; it is possible, indeed, for the Creed to be said immediately after the sermon. The version of the Nicene Creed printed in THE SUNDAY SERVICE is a new translation made by the International Consultation on English

THE SUNDAY SERVICE (2)

Texts, which has commended itself to other denominations also.

We are now approaching the most important part of the service—the section which reflects the words and actions of our Lord at the Last Supper. In the Upper Room, Jesus did seven things:

1. He took bread
2. He gave thanks
3. He broke the bread
4. He gave the bread to his disciples
5. He took the cup
6. He gave thanks
7. He gave the wine to his disciples.

These seven actions may conveniently be reduced to four:

1. He took the bread and the wine
2. He gave thanks
3. He broke the bread
4. He gave the bread and the wine to his disciples

THE SUNDAY SERVICE now models its structure upon those four actions. Many liturgists believe that the 'Four-Action Shape' is the traditional form of the Eucharist; others, it is true, are not convinced by this theory.[1] THE SUNDAY SERVICE, however, like many other rites, is structured in this way; and, in consequence, it effectively represents the deeds of our Lord.

[1] See, for example, the Joint Liturgical Group's publication, *Initiation and Eucharist*, SPCK, 1972, pp. 24 f.

1. He took Bread and Wine: the Setting of the Table

The first action of Jesus is re-enacted in the Setting of the Table. Ideally the elements (bread and wine) will have been left in another place—the vestry or the vestibule, perhaps—so that at this point they can be brought to the minister, together with the gifts of money that have previously been collected. This is a fine piece of symbolism; representatives of the worshipping community bring forward money, bread and wine as a symbol of the congregation's self-offering; these ordinary things will be transformed by God. Alternatively, if the elements are already on the Table, they are now uncovered, and if the collection has not previously been brought forward, it is now presented. The minister, representing Christ at the Last Supper, takes the bread and the wine and prepares them for use.

2. He Gave Thanks: The Thanksgiving

The second action of Jesus is reflected in the Thanksgiving. We have no means of knowing what our Lord said when he gave thanks, but over the centuries, great prayers of thanksgiving have come to have certain characteristic features. The prayer begins with *Sursum Corda* ('Lift up your hearts'), a traditional dialogue between minister and congregation. Then there is a fine summary of the mighty acts of God in creation and redemption; the foundation of Christian belief is expressed in these few sentences, which repay careful study. This recital of what God has done for us (known to liturgists as 'the Preface') leads the congregation to join in an 'unending hymn of praise' in

THE SUNDAY SERVICE (2)

the words of the *Sanctus* ('Holy, holy, holy Lord'). This is said 'with all the company of heaven'; in their worship, Christians recognize a link between the constant act of worship offered in heaven and its counterparts on earth. Every service, however small the congregation, is part of the continual act of worship of the Church 'militant and triumphant'.

Thanksgiving is now related to the institution of the Eucharist at the Last Supper. The Words of Institution have traditionally been considered one of the most vital parts of the Eucharist; indeed, some Christians would say that it is by the reading of these words that the bread and the wine are consecrated. We need not commit ourselves to this view to see that the Words of Institution are a perpetual reminder that our celebration of the Lord's Supper is a re-enactment of what Christ and his disciples did at the Last Supper.

The congregation now joins in a short statement of faith and hope:

> 'Christ has died.
> Christ is risen.
> Christ will come again.'

This is a joyful statement, and it should sound joyful. Words like these deserve to be shouted!

The great prayer now states that the sacrament is being celebrated in remembrance of Christ, in obedience to his command. This statement is called *anamnesis* ('memorial'). Next we ask God to accept our sacrifice of praise and thanksgiving, thus offering to him our worship itself. *Epiklesis* follows; this is a petition that, through the power of the Holy Spirit, 'we who receive your gifts of bread and wine may share in the body and blood of Christ', and be made 'one body with him'. Then we offer ourselves as a living sacrifice, as we have previously offered our worship.

The great prayer ends with a 'doxology', an ascription of glory, said by the whole congregation. In the experimental version of THE SUNDAY SERVICE, equivalent words were said by the minister alone: the final rite improves upon this by involving all the worshippers. The doxology is a splendid conclusion to the prayer, and it is not a passage to be mumbled. It should raise the roof!

3. He Broke the Bread: The Breaking of the Bread

Jesus's third action is represented when the minister 'breaks the bread in the sight of the people'. This can be a most impressive act if it is performed well. The minister should not fumble inconspicuously over the Table; nor should members of the congregation bury their heads in their service books or assume an attitude of prayer. The minister cannot manage with a crumb; he needs a large piece of bread to break, and he should extend the pieces at arms' length, while the congregation watches attentively. The action may be performed in silence, or one of three sets of responsive sentences may be said. The third action is a fine piece of liturgical drama.

The congregation now sits or kneels, and silence is kept during which worshippers make their own

THE SUNDAY SERVICE (2)

prayerful preparation before receiving the bread and the wine.

4. He Gave Bread and Wine to His Disciples: The Sharing of the Bread and Wine

The fourth action of Jesus is represented when his contemporary disciples share the bread and the wine. The action is delayed, however, if the Prayer of Humble Access is said. This prayer, now presented in modern English, has held an honoured place in almost all Anglican and Methodist eucharistic rites; but it introduces a note of penitence and provokes a sense of unworthiness that is not entirely appropriate after so joyous a great prayer of thanksgiving. It is perhaps wisest, therefore, to omit it, except on penitential occasions such as Sundays in Lent.

After the minister and any who are assisting him have received the bread and wine, the whole congregation receives the elements. A period of silence follows, during which all may pray or meditate. Then a short thanksgiving for what has happened is said; this short prayer fittingly expresses our gratitude for what has been done for us in the Eucharist.

A hymn may be sung, and a blessing may be said. Congregations are accustomed to the saying of a blessing at the end of every service, but it can be argued that, after we have received the body and blood of Christ, we require no further blessing. Even if the blessing is said, that is not the end of the service. For the minister now exhorts the congregation to 'Go in peace in the power of the Spirit to live and work to God's praise and glory', and the congregation responds, 'Thanks be to God'. This is an excellent way to end the service, a reminder that worship leads to service, the living out of the Faith in daily life.

Celebration

Readers may have noticed that the word 'celebration' has been used several times in this chapter and is employed in THE SUNDAY SERVICE itself. 'Celebration' is a concept which has been strongly emphasized by the Liturgical Movement. The word is rich in meaning and association; in the context of worship it means far more than its use in everyday life would suggest.[2] Yet it includes everything that we normally associate with celebration—gaiety, joy, festivity. Worship can be compared with a party held in someone's honour or to commemorate a specific event; in worship we celebrate the mighty acts of God; we celebrate his presence with us; we rejoice and express our gratitude to him. The Eucharist is the supreme Christian party, and as we celebrate, Christ is mysteriously present as both host and guest:

'Come, risen Lord, and deign to be our guest;
Nay, let us be thy guests: the feast is thine...'[3]

It is unfortunate that so many of us have been conditioned to think of the Lord's Supper as an occasion for special penitence; it is sad that so many worshippers come to the communion rail with long

---

[2] For a detailed account of the meaning of 'Celebration', see P. F. Bradshaw's article in R. C. D. Jasper (ed.), *The Eucharist Today*, SPCK, 1974, pp. 130–41.
[3] *Hymns and Songs* 13.

THE SUNDAY SERVICE (2)

faces. For, in truth, there is no occasion more joyous than this, more deserving of a happy smile. The Eucharist is 'a foretaste of the heavenly banquet prepared for all mankind'. THE SUNDAY SERVICE, which reflects the concepts of thanksgiving and celebration much more clearly than any previous Methodist rite, should help us to overcome some of our inhibitions, and to celebrate as we ought.

Questions for discussion

1. How would the congregation of your church react to the giving of the Peace by means of a handclasp?

2. Discuss the dramatic qualities of the Lord's Supper —especially the Peace, the Setting of the Table, the Breaking of the Bread, and the Sharing of the Bread and Wine—in the light of the comment that 'worship should appeal to all the senses, not just to the sense of hearing'.

3. Read the great prayer of thanksgiving slowly, pausing after each paragraph to discuss its contents.

4. Should the Prayer of Humble Access normally be included in the Eucharist, or is it better to omit it? Give reasons for your answer.

4 The Sunday Service (3)

However much importance we attach to the Eucharist, we must recognize that there is no prospect of its weekly celebration becoming the norm in Methodism in the near future. This is partly because less frequent celebration has been common practice for so long that many people would resist change; and partly because of the simple administrative difficulty in many circuits of supplying enough ministers to preside. So guidance is offered in *The Methodist Service Book* to ministers and local preachers in the conduct of services without the Lord's Supper.

'In many churches of the Reformation tradition it has been the custom, once on a Sunday, for the shape of the service to reflect that of the complete order of Word and Sacrament even when there is no celebration of the Lord's Supper.'[1] As a guide for this purpose an outline form of service is provided, together with explanatory notes. This outline is divided into three parts:

The Preparation
The Ministry of the Word
The Response.

1. The Preparation

It is suggested that the service should begin with a

[1] THE SUNDAY SERVICE WITHOUT THE LORD'S SUPPER, introduction.

THE SUNDAY SERVICE (3)

hymn and a group of prayers. Such an opening rite is not new; Methodist services have almost invariably begun in this way for many years. Here, and wherever prayer is suggested, it may be offered extempore. The tradition of extempore prayer (offered spontaneously rather than written down in advance or read from a book) has an honourable history in Methodism, and at its best it can bring freshness and vitality to worship. At its worst, of course, it can spoil services. Formal prayer, on the other hand, was valued by John Wesley, and, as we have noticed, this part of our heritage has never been wholly lost. Wesley sensibly made use of both formal and extempore prayer; and his example is worth following.

The Preparation should include two important elements of worship. The first, *adoration*, expresses the sense of wonder and reverence which we feel when we are confronted by the majestic fact of God. There are many hymns of adoration; and if one of these is sung, there is no need to include adoration in the prayer. The second element of worship is *confession*; this arises naturally from adoration, for, in the light of God's majesty and love, our own unworthiness is clearly revealed. The printed prayer of confession may be read; there should be a declaration of God's forgiveness. (This is too often forgotten; the Gospel not only convicts men of their sin: it assures them of God's forgiving love.)

There is a good deal to be gained by reading the Collect of the Day among the opening prayers, especially if the readings which follow are taken from the lectionary. Consistent use of the collects, whether or not there is a celebration of the Lord's Supper, enables the congregation to become familiar with them all.

2. The Ministry of the Word

This section of the service consists mainly of Bible readings and a sermon. The use of the readings provided in COLLECTS, LESSONS AND PSALMS is 'strongly commended'. What we have said about collects applies with even greater force to lessons; the use of the lectionary in every service, whether or not there is a celebration of the Lord's Supper, gives congregations an opportunity to hear a wide selection of Scripture passages. It is recommended that there should be either an Old Testament lesson or an Epistle, or both, plus a Gospel reading. Hymns may be inserted before the first lesson and before the Gospel.

The reading of Scripture is so much a part of the pattern of worship which we have inherited that it might seem unnecessary to ask why it is included in this outline—and indeed in every other service in *The Methodist Service Book*. Many preachers, however, can testify to the strange lack of attentiveness that seems to come over congregations during Bible readings. In part this lack of interest may sometimes be due to obscure readings, couched in the archaic language of the Authorized Version, and badly delivered; but even when these obstacles are removed, the words of Wesley do not often ring true: '... in Thy word we search for Thee—We search with trembling awe...'.

THE SUNDAY SERVICE (3)

Undoubtedly, the remoteness of many biblical concepts from those of our own day contributes to the problem. New translations, however excellent, cannot by themselves help worshippers to understand notions such as 'covenant', 'sacrifice', 'justification' or Saint John's specialized use of 'the Word'. Here the task of the preacher in expounding the Scriptures is shown to be vital. But why, in any case, should congregations be encouraged to treat Bible readings as important?

It is the Church's belief that God has revealed himself to men, chiefly through his Son, Jesus Christ. The Bible is no longer considered by the majority of Christians to be an infallible oracle, but it is still recognized as a supreme witness to God's acts of self-revelation. Through reading and studying the Scriptures, men can, as it were, hear God speaking to them. Thus Bible readings are included in worship, not because of their academic interest, but because through them we hope to hear God speaking to us. God can and does speak to men in other ways; but we impoverish worship if we do not make good use of Bible readings as vehicles for the voice of God.

When congregations approach the reading of Scripture in this light, this part of worship becomes much more significant. There are several means of bringing readings to life: passages can be read by members of the congregation; some can be split into sections for a number of readers—the Passion narratives, for instance, respond well to this treatment; worshippers can be encouraged to follow the lessons while they are being read, using their own Bibles. It is also noteworthy that such methods allow for active congregational participation, which is a virtue in itself.

The sermon follows the readings. In Chapter Two, we defended sermons on the ground that the Word of God which has been read requires to be expounded. Occasionally, it may be felt that this exposition can be presented more effectively in other ways—films, colour slides, interviews, for example—and while THE SUNDAY SERVICE does not suggest such variations, it does not preclude them. But for the most part, sermons will be accepted as the normal means of expounding the Scriptures. This is an important part of worship, one which shows the relevance of the biblical revelation to the life of the modern world, and which challenges Christians to live out their faith in that world.

But in stressing the importance of sermons, we must be careful not to exaggerate. For too long, the sermon has been thought to be the grand climax of every act of worship; and even today, we sometimes hear the rest of the service described as 'the preliminaries'. The implication of this is clear: the main reason for coming to church is to hear a sermon; all else leads up to that. This is a most inadequate view of worship. Worship is communion with God, celebration of God's presence, celebration of his mighty acts, and more. It is not just a matter of listening to sermons, however moving or instructive some sermons may be.

The sermon then needs to be seen not as the 'top of the bill', but as an integrated part of the whole act of worship. It must be related to the readings and must therefore 'be so placed as to make clear its link with the Scriptures from which it arises'.[2] That is why, in this outline, the sermon comes about half-way through the service, instead of almost at the end. The practice of separating the sermon from the readings by notices and collection, a prayer and a couple of hymns, has nothing to commend it, although it still lingers on in many churches. It is a survival of the exaggerated view of the importance of sermons; it is to be hoped that THE SUNDAY SERVICE will hasten it towards its long overdue death. Not only does it obscure the unity of readings and sermon; but it also tends to limit response after the sermon to a single hymn—and this is most inadequate.

In any one service, the readings and the sermon will focus attention on one or two aspects of Christian belief or behaviour. In the course of time, if the lectionary is used, all major aspects will be covered, but in a single service this is clearly impossible. For that reason it is good that we should be reminded that what we have heard is only part of a whole. The Apostles' Creed, which summarizes the major elements of the Christian Faith, helps us to do this. The reading of the Creed, followed by a hymn, concludes the Ministry of the Word.

3. The Response
In worship, as we have said, God speaks to us (proclamation) and we speak to God (response). It is not possible to distinguish completely between the

[2] General Directions.

two parts of this conversation. Even during readings and sermons, which might be thought to belong clearly to the category 'God speaks to us', worshippers make a response of some sort in their hearts. But in general terms we can usefully make a distinction between acts of proclamation and acts of response; and this is done in THE SUNDAY SERVICE by grouping together the former in the Ministry of the Word and the latter in the Response.

The Response begins with prayer. *Thanksgiving* flows naturally from the proclamation of the Word of God, for the good news of what God has done for mankind in Christ leads us to gratitude. It is a great pity that this element of worship is so frequently neglected. THE SUNDAY SERVICE provides five prayers of thanksgiving and dedication, all of which, while allowing ample scope for variation, include thanksgiving for the mighty acts of God. *Intercession* follows. As we have seen, prayer for others is another vital element in a full act of worship; it is the liturgical expression of the concern which Christians feel for the salvation of all mankind. Here again, five forms of prayer are supplied.

It is suggested that these prayers of thanksgiving and intercession should reach their climax in the Lord's Prayer. Although many Methodist congregations normally say this prayer after the first prayer of the service—in the Preparation—there is no sound liturgical reason for this practice; it dates from a time when there was usually only one prayer in any one service. It seems more fitting, in fact, to recite the

THE SUNDAY SERVICE (3)

prayer which Jesus taught his disciples as an act of response—and, indeed, as the climax of response.

The service ends with a hymn and either a dismissal or a blessing, or both. A blessing is normal in most services; but the more challenging words of the dismissal, with their reminder that good worship leads to Christian service, may be more appropriate on most occasions.

No special place is assigned to the notices and the collection. Local customs, problems caused by the arrival or departure of children, and other factors make it difficult to give precise guidelines on this point. In any case, what liturgical function do these elements of worship fulfil? The notices, for instance, can be described as an act of proclamation: this, we are saying, is what God is doing in this place. But equally, they can be described as an act of response: as a result of what we have heard, this is what we local Christians are going to do. The best position for the notices, however, is not the most urgent problem to confront the modern Church, and there is no need to make a mountain out of this molehill. The notices can be inserted at any point where they do not interrupt the flow of the service. In any case, there is no difficulty at all if they are duplicated or printed—a practice that is becoming widespread.

The collection poses greater problems. The present writer subscribes to the view that the offering of the congregation's gifts of money is a symbol of total dedication, and is best included in the Response, before the thanksgiving prayer, or after the Lord's Prayer, or during the final hymn. The gifts should be brought forward, the congregation standing. The offering of money can then symbolize something greater; and its position roughly corresponds with the Setting of the Table in the Lord's Supper. But a different view has recently been cogently argued by Dr David Stacey, who believes that the 'natural break' at the end of the Preparation is the most opportune time for the offering. Dr Stacey would like to abolish the procession of stewards and the dedicatory prayer, 'for we do not really believe in a ritual dedication of money, we do not want to give the money that much prominence, and we do want to make an offering of ourselves, which includes our money, later in the programme'.[3] Local churches must decide for themselves between these two opinions.

By now, readers will have made their own comparisons between the form of preaching service which has been familiar for several generations and the outline suggested in THE SUNDAY SERVICE. They will have noticed in the latter a clear development from one act of worship to the next, a logical structure, and an overall shape which reflects that of the full order of Word and Sacrament. From time to time, it will no doubt be necessary to use different types of structure; but where a 'normal order of service' is required, THE SUNDAY SERVICE provides one which is as good as any, and better than most.

Questions for discussion
1. Do you agree that the outline suggested in THE

[3] John Stacey (ed.), *About Worship*, Preachers' Handbook (New Series) Number 4, p. 64.

THE SUNDAY SERVICE (3)

SUNDAY SERVICE 'is as good as any, and better than most for normal use?

2. Should a local church try to impose a pattern of worship upon those who conduct worship there?

3. Do you agree that sermons have been over-emphasized? Discuss the relationship between sermons and other acts of worship.

4. Using the outline as a basis, draft out a service including the lectionary readings for any Sunday. Choose appropriate hymns and prayers, and fit in other elements of worship (e.g. notices, offering, anthem) at suitable places.

5 The Baptism of Infants

Most denominations, including Methodism, baptize infants. This has long been so; but the circumstances in which the Church finds itself in these days are causing some Christians to become dissatisfied with the traditional practice. For only a tiny minority of the population practises Christianity; and most parents who present their children for baptism do not belong to this minority. Some people, therefore, hope that eventually the custom of baptizing the children of non-Christian parents (or, indeed, any children) will be discontinued. Others would deplore such a change; the debate goes on. It is extremely probable, however, that for the foreseeable future, Methodism's general practice will remain the same.

Baptism is the first part of entry into the Church. The second part, confirmation, takes place when a person baptized in infancy is able to answer for himself and has responded to the call of Christ. He then voluntarily ratifies what was done on his behalf years before, and the Church prays that he may be strengthened by the Holy Spirit for Christian service.

A baptized child is a member of the Church, but not a full member. His membership is, in a sense, conditional until it is endorsed by his own action and that of the Church in confirmation. In this chapter we are concerned with baptism; in Chapter 6 we shall consider confirmation.

THE BAPTISM OF INFANTS

A few years ago, baptism was often administered at times other than the normal hours of worship, usually in the afternoon or after morning service. This was a bad practice: it separated the children who were baptized from the worshipping community of which, by baptism, they were made members. The recognition that baptism is an act in which the whole local Church family should share has led to an increase in the number of baptisms administered during principal services. Our new baptismal service is designed to fit into the framework of THE SUNDAY SERVICE, either early in the service or after the sermon.

The service has six sections:

1. The Preparation
2. The Ministry of the Word
3. The Baptismal Prayer
4. The Promises and the Profession of Faith
5. The Baptism
6. The Final Prayers.

1. The Preparation
The Lord's Prayer is said, unless it is to be said later, and any other part of the Preparation of THE SUNDAY SERVICE may be used. Then follows the Collect of the Day, or some other prayer, or a special baptismal collect.

2. The Ministry of the Word
The General Directions give detailed guidance about the choice of Bible readings. It is normally desirable that the service at which baptism takes place should

have its own lessons (preferably those appointed in the lectionary), though occasionally a whole series of readings on baptism may be appropriate. The order advocated in THE BAPTISM OF INFANTS is theologically very sound. Baptism is a response to the Word of God: the New Testament tells of men hearing the Word of God expounded, responding to it, and being baptized. So ideally an Old Testament Lesson or an Epistle are read, and a sermon preached. Then three short passages from the Gospels are read, followed by a brief exposition which is printed in the order of service. Response to these readings and expositions logically follows in prayer, promises, and the act of baptism.

But sometimes, practical considerations may cause the first reading and the sermon to be deferred until after the baptismal service is complete. The essential principle is preserved, however, for the Gospel passages are read, together with the printed exposition. Thus the Word is proclaimed before the act of response begins.

3. The Baptismal Prayer

The baptismal prayer begins with thanksgiving. This is a high point in the service, for thanksgiving is the heart of worship. This prayer is an echo of the great prayer of thanksgiving in THE SUNDAY SERVICE. Thanksgiving is offered for creation and redemption: in particular, that Christ is our Saviour, that he has broken the power of evil; and that he has sent the Holy Spirit to make us a new creation. These themes are reflected in the second part of the prayer, which

THE BAPTISM OF INFANTS

consists of petitions for the child. We pray that he may die to sin and be raised to the new life; that he may learn to trust Jesus as his Lord and Saviour; that he may have victory over evil; and that from darkness he may be led to light.

This prayer expresses a number of important aspects of the theology of baptism. Baptism is a divine act of new creation; it proclaims the saving love of God; it declares God's power to deal with human sin and to break the power of evil.

4. The Promises and the Profession of Faith

Infants cannot speak. It is fitting, therefore, that the adults present should make certain promises. The parents, who will be most concerned with the Christian upbringing of the child, and who will exert the strongest influences upon him, are asked to make three promises. Theirs is the heaviest responsibility. But the local community of Christians, who are to receive the child in Christ's name, are reminded of their responsibility by being asked to make a promise of their own—that they will 'so maintain the common life of worship and service that he ... may grow in grace and in the knowledge and love of God and of his Son Jesus Christ our Lord'.

Then follow the promises of the parents. It is stated in the General Directions that if parents cannot pledge themselves to give these promises, the baptism of their child may be deferred. This indicates the importance which is attached to the parents' promises. Parents do not always recognize that, in presenting their children for baptism, they take upon themselves serious responsibilities; they are pledged to bring up their children 'in the nurture and admonition of the Lord' (General Directions). As a sign of their intention to do this, they are asked to give three promises: to provide for their children Christian homes of love and faithfulness; to help them by their words, prayers and example to renounce all evil and to put their trust in Jesus Christ their Saviour; and to encourage them to enter into the full membership of the Church and to serve Christ in the world.

The 1936 baptismal service made no provision for godparents; in Methodism it has always been recognized that the influence of parents is of paramount importance. But in the new service, a promise is included for 'sponsors'. Two sponsors may, if it is desired, be appointed to assist the parents in carrying out their promises—one chosen by the parents themselves, and the other, normally a member of the church in which the baptism takes place, by the minister. In theory, the idea of a sponsor provided by the church is good; but some churches may well find difficulty in supplying such sponsors, especially if baptisms are held frequently; while some parents may resist the practice for reasons of their own.

After the sponsors have promised to support the parents in the Christian upbringing of the child, the minister invites the congregation to 'confess the faith of the Church'. This is done by the recitation of either the Apostles' Creed (in the new translation prepared by the International Consultation on English Texts) or a short summary of it.

It seems to have been the practice of the Early

THE BAPTISM OF INFANTS

Church to ask candidates for baptism three questions, similar in scope to the short summary. (The first would be: 'Do you believe in God the Father almighty?') After each answer, the candidate would be immersed in water. From these questions and answers, which became extended as time passed, the Apostles' Creed developed. It is, therefore, very appropriate that either the Creed or the summary should be said at this point, as a proclamation of what the Church believes, before the child is baptized into this Faith.

5. The Baptism

The parents formally present their child for baptism and, after the minister has taken him into his arms, they name the child. Then the minister baptizes him in water, in the names of the Person of the Trinity. The minister makes the sign of the cross on the forehead of the child, saying, 'By Baptism we receive this child into the congregation of Christ's flock...' Then —and this is an innovation—the whole congregation joins the minister in saying the 'Aaronic Blessing' (Numbers 6:24–26). Previously only the minister said these words; the new rubric allows everyone present to welcome the child into the family of the Church.

The giving of a lighted candle is optional, which is perhaps just as well, because this ceremony has already attracted a good deal of controversy. The practice is new to Methodism, although some baptismal rites have included it for centuries. In some minds, there is a fear of the trappings of 'High Churchmanship', and suspicion that the introduction of a candle portends an unholy alliance with Rome. Simply because the ceremony is unprecedented in Methodism, some worshippers object to it. This is unfortunate: the symbolism of the candle is clearly brought out in the words that accompany its giving ('I give you this sign, for you now belong to Christ, the light of the world', 'Let your light so shine before men...'). If the giving of the candle is regarded with an unprejudiced eye, this symbolism is seen to be full of meaning.

6. The Final Prayers
A prayer for the child, his family, and the Church now follows; the baptismal service then concludes with the Grace. The rubrics indicate how the main service should continue.

Questions for discussion
1. Should the practice of baptizing infants be discontinued?

2. Discuss, sentence by sentence, the prayer on p. A8 which the minister says.

3. Comment on the promises made by the congregation, the parents, and the sponsors, saying in particular whether you think the right questions are asked.

4. Discuss the giving of the lighted candle, and give reasons for your attitude to this practice.

6 Confirmation

'Those who have by Baptism been admitted into the visible community of the Church are constantly to be taught to look forward to their reception into the full membership of the Church, when by professing their faith in Christ they will claim for themselves the promises of God, who by his Holy Spirit will strengthen them for his service.'[1] It is unfortunately true that the majority of people baptized as infants never present themselves for confirmation; but every year, the Methodist Church makes a good number of new members in confirmation services. Confirmation is the second part of entry into the Church, the sequel to baptism.

The confirmation service follows a period of training, during which candidates are taught the main doctrines and practices of the Christian Church; and the local church authorities must be satisfied that the candidates meet the requirements which the Methodist Church lays down. The service is held in conjunction with the Lord's Supper. It has four sections:

The Ministry of the Word
The Promises and the Profession of Faith
The Confirmation and Reception
The Lord's Supper.

[1] PUBLIC RECEPTION INTO FULL MEMBERSHIP, OR CONFIRMATION, General Directions.

1. The Ministry of the Word

The service begins with a hymn—either 'In the name of Jesus' or another hymn—and a special confirmation collect or extempore prayer. Then follow the Old Testament lesson and the Epistle, as set out in the printed service, except at certain great festivals when the lessons of the day take precedence. A hymn, 'Christ, from whom all blessings flow', or some other, leads to the Gospel—from Mark 1, except at the festivals—and the sermon.

Once again we see how good liturgy follows the logic of theology. Despite some appearances to the contrary, the Church is not a club which a man may join if he feels like it, and from which he may sever his connection at will. To belong to the Church is to have responded to the call of Christ. 'Jesus said to them, "Follow me".' His call comes to us; then we respond, for him or against him. This is the heart of confirmation theology: Jesus calls us to accept a place in his family, a place that has been reserved for us since we were baptized; we respond to that call; the Church publicly recognizes our response and admits us to the full membership of the family; by his Holy Spirit God strengthens us (confirms us) for his service.

This theology is reflected in the structure of the confirmation service. The Ministry of the Word, in readings and sermon, represents the call of Christ. It is the proclamation to which we respond.

After the sermon, a hymn is sung—'O Thou who camest from above' is recommended. Then those who are to be confirmed stand, and the minister addresses them, relating the theology of baptism and confirmation to their own experience. This brings the Ministry of the Word to an end.

2. The Promises and the Profession of Faith

A section of response now follows. This partly represents the candidates' general response to the call of Christ; it is also the embodiment of a specific part of that call—the invitation to become full members of the Church. The candidates are asked three questions, which are closely related to the second and third promises given by parents in baptism:

Baptism
2. Will you help him by your words, prayers and example to renounce all evil and to put his trust in Jesus Christ his Saviour?
3. Will you encourage him to enter into the full membership of the Church and to serve Christ in the world?

Confirmation
1. Do you repent of your sins and renounce all evil?
2. Do you trust in Jesus Christ as your Lord and Saviour?
3. Will you obey Christ and serve him in the Church and in the world?

When these questions have been answered, the whole congregation recites the Apostles' Creed: this is another parallel between baptism and confirmation. The Creed is a summary of the Faith of the Church, into the full membership of which the candidates are about to be received.

3. The Confirmation and Reception

This part of the service begins with prayer; while the congregation remains standing and the candidates kneel, the minister prays that the candidates may be established in faith by the Holy Spirit, and equipped with spiritual gifts.

The ancient practice of laying on of hands is associated with many rites, not least with ordination, confirmation, and healing services. In the case of confirmation, denominational opinion varies as to the necessity of the laying on of hands for the validity of the rite. Anglicans and Roman Catholics, for example, consider it indispensable, while many Free Churches do not practise it at all. The Methodist Church does not consider the laying on of hands to be vital in confirmation—people were received into the full membership of the Church for very many years without it—but Methodism does believe that the action is fitting. In order to make this clear, and to accommodate those who do not greatly like the practice, two forms of confirmation and reception are provided, only one of which requires the laying on of hands.

In the first form, the minister lays his hands upon the head of each candidate, saying the prayer of confirmation, 'Lord, confirm your servant N. by your Holy Spirit that he may continue yours for ever', and each candidate replies 'Amen'. Then all stand, and the minister welcomes those who have now become members of the Church universal and local; he and a representative member of the local church may give the right hand of fellowship to each candidate.

CONFIRMATION

The alternative form places greater emphasis on the welcome and the right hand of fellowship. Without laying on his hands, the minister says the prayer of confirmation once only, for all the candidates together. Then each candidate is individually welcomed and given the right hand of fellowship by the minister (and, if desired, by a representative of the local church).

Whichever method is used, the idea of a lay representative joining the minister in welcoming the new full members is good. The minister is, by virtue of his ordination, a representative of the wider family of the Church; a local layman, although himself part of the wider community, represents the local church more directly, and his participation embodies the principle that the whole local community is involved in the reception of new members.

Many churches make some sort of presentation to those who have been confirmed, as a token of their welcome and as a memento of the occasion, and provision is made in the service for a Bible or some other book to be given to them at this point. Then the congregation joins in a short prayer of dedication, which quotes from THE COVENANT SERVICE and directs the congregation's thoughts outwards—into the world. This is as it should be. The Church should not be inward-looking; it should be a body of men and women committed to Christ and concerned to 'serve (their) neighbours and to bring them to believe in him'. The Lord's Prayer is said, and the hymn, 'Lord, in the strength of grace', which was also in the 1936 service, is sung.

4. The Lord's Supper

Directions are now given for the transition to THE SUNDAY SERVICE. The minister begins at the Setting of the Table; a hymn, 'Ye servants of God', is suggested for use after communion.

This is a fine service, much to be preferred to its predecessor of 1936, which was spoiled by its inordinate length—it was intended to be used 'at the close of a shortened service on the Lord's Day'—and its verbosity. The new service has many merits; not least is its ability to link the act of confirmation both with baptism, by means of its frequent references to and parallels with that rite, and with the ongoing life of the Church, in its emphasis on service and its close association with the Eucharist.

The Baptism of Those who are Able to Answer for Themselves with the Public Reception into Full Membership or Confirmation

It sometimes happens that a person wishes to be confirmed who has not been baptized in infancy. In this event, a special form of service is used, and, unless there is good reason for separating the two, this service includes both baptism and confirmation. Because this sort of service is not required frequently, we have followed *The Methodist Service Book* in dealing with it after infant baptism and confirmation, but historically and theologically, adult baptism is the norm. The Early Church generally administered baptism and confirmation together to adult converts; infant baptism was a later concession to Christian parents. Thus it is entirely right, as well as convenient,

CONFIRMATION

that when an adult is baptized he should at the same time be confirmed.

The service combines the principal elements of the baptism and confirmation services:

The Ministry of the Word
The Baptismal Prayer
The Promises and the Profession of Faith
The Baptism
The Confirmation and Reception
The Lord's Supper.

With two exceptions, the suggested hymns are different from those in the confirmation service. In the Ministry of the Word, a special collect, suitable for adult baptism, is provided, and different lessons are also supplied. The minister's statement at the end of this section is also of necessity different from that in THE BAPTISM OF INFANTS. The baptismal prayer covers the same ground, though at greater length. The promise of the congregation is suitably changed. Those who are to be baptized (and others who, having been baptized previously, are to be confirmed) are asked the questions printed in the confirmation service. The Apostles' Creed is said. The Baptism section is confined to the naming of the candidates and the application of water to them, together with the minister's declaration of baptism.

If there are any candidates for confirmation who have previously been baptized, the minister addresses them in the words which include the Ministry of the Word in the confirmation service. The confirmation service, beginning with the prayer for those about to be confirmed, now follows, and leads into the Lord's Supper at the Setting of the Table.

Appendix A
In exceptional circumstances, confirmation may not immediately follow baptism. In this case, after applying water to the candidate, the minister makes the sign of the cross on his forehead, saying substantially the same words as are said in THE BAPTISM OF INFANTS at this point; and the congregation says the Aaronic Blessing. Then the minister says a short prayer for the person newly baptized, and the Grace.

Appendix B
The second appendix gives directions for the reception of Christians of other communions into the full membership of the Methodist Church. Particularly noteworthy are the provisions for the reception of confirmed Christians of denominations from which they cannot be received by transfer. After suitable preparation has taken place, such people may be publicly received, after the sermon, during a celebration of the Eucharist, by stating that they desire to take up the duties and privileges of membership, and being welcomed by the minister with the right hand of fellowship, followed by prayer.

Questions for discussion
1. A few years ago, people were often received into the full membership of the Church without any service of public reception. Do you think it right that this practice is now discouraged?

CONFIRMATION

2. Discuss the meaning of full membership in terms of the statement on p. A21.

3. Compare the alternative forms of confirmation and reception on pp. A23 f; say which you prefer and why.

4. Do you think that Methodism places enough emphasis upon confirmation?

7 The Covenant Service

The word 'commitment' is rather overworked, but the idea which it expresses is vitally important in the Christian life. Being a Christian is no hobby or pastime; it is a total life-style. Jesus does not ask us for part of our lives, nor even for large sections of them; he invites us to follow him without reserve, to commit ourselves to him completely. Followers of Jesus are committed to several things, not the least of which is worship; but worship is not only part of our commitment: it is also a means of strengthening and deepening our entire commitment. Most of the services in *The Methodist Service Book* are concerned with some aspect of the Christian commitment, and of this THE COVENANT SERVICE is a prime example.

Services for the Renewal of the Covenant have been held by Methodists since the time of John Wesley, who found that they were effective means of grace for many people. Wesley modelled his Covenant Services on the work of Nonconformist writers of the seventeenth century, but the history of such services takes us much further back than that. There is evidence that services for Covenant renewal were a feature of early Hebrew worship; and undoubtedly 'Covenant' is one of the major themes of the Bible. The word 'testament', indeed, means 'covenant'—a fact which suggests the importance of the concept.

The ancient nation of Israel believed that it had a

THE COVENANT SERVICE

special relationship with God, based on a Covenant agreement, made first between God and Abraham, and subsequently confirmed with others, notably Moses. The terms of the Covenant were clear; on the one hand, God would surround his people with love, care and protection: on the other, the nation would remain loyal to God, worshipping him alone and obeying his laws. If the people failed to keep their part of the agreement, they would be liable to God's punishment: to violate the Covenant was to court disaster. Again and again in the writings of the prophets and in the books associated with the 'Deuteronomic School',[1] national disasters are attributed to the people's disobedience to the laws of the Covenant God, whereas prosperity is seen as a direct result of faithfulness to the Covenant. The nation had a corporate responsibility for keeping the Covenant, by which every Israelite was bound. Disobedience could lead to the punishment of the whole nation, even, so it was believed, affecting future generations. Children could be punished for their fathers' sins.

While retaining a firm hold on the Covenant idea, the great prophet, Jeremiah, was repelled by the notion that sin could be punished corporately, innocent and guilty suffering the same fate. Jeremiah envisaged a new sort of Covenant; the law of God would be implanted in individual hearts, and each person would be responsible for his own actions, individually accountable to God. This belief, of course, takes no account of the complex relationship between

[1] Deuteronomy, Joshua, Judges, I and II Samuel, I and II Kings.

individual and corporate sin; but Jeremiah's vision[2] of a new Covenant based upon an inward relationship with God rather than on formal external observance, is a masterpiece of the Old Testament.

In the New Testament, the Christian Church is described as the New Israel, and Jesus is referred to as the mediator of a New Covenant, founded on the love of God revealed in him and on the faith of those who believe in him. Although there is often no direct allusion to the Covenant, many ideas associated with this theme are employed in the New Testament; there are reminders about the special calling of Christians, exhortations to remain loyal to Christ, and warnings about the dangers of deserting the cause of Jesus.

That Covenant is an important biblical theme is not open to question; it is equally evident that Covenant Services are a significant part of the Methodist heritage. But is 'Covenant' still a meaningful concept? Some would think that it is not. We are all familiar, of course, with the signing of contracts and the making of business deals; but can the Christian's relationship with God be compared with these agreements? Is it not rather offensive to suggest that it can?

Certainly, it is poor theology to think that the relationship bears any resemblance to the dealings that take place between City magnates; God and man are not equals, or almost equals: the initiative comes from God, without whom man is powerless. The bond is not made for mutual advantage; it is God's gift, an expression of his love for man and his desire

[2] Jeremiah 31:29–34.

THE COVENANT SERVICE

to live in communion with him. Nor can the relationship be seen in purely mechanical or legalistic terms, for it depends on the interaction of the living God with living human beings: it is not static; it is dynamic.

Even so, the Covenant idea is not without meaning. The Bible records the conviction of the two great religions of Judaism and Christianity that God in his mercy does desire close relationships with people. No one can deserve such favour: it is bestowed regardless of our deserts—but it does impose obligations upon us. We must cease to imagine that we are our own masters—'I am no longer my own, but yours'. The relationship between God and man is both corporate and individual; the individual can know the love of God and is personally accountable to God, but his response must be expressed not only privately but also in the fellowship of the Church, which corporately enjoys a special relationship with God. The Covenant theme effectively expresses these convictions.

But are Covenant Services either necessary or desirable? David Tripp, in his admirable account of the Covenant Service in Methodism,[3] has listed a number of adverse criticisms of the Covenant Service levelled by writers since the time of Wesley. The most important of these are as follows:

1. Covenant Services are too intensely personal in tone to be used publicly. They may have their place

[3] David Tripp, *The Renewal of the Covenant in the Methodist Tradition*, Epworth Press, 1969.

in private devotion, but they are inappropriate as acts of corporate worship. This criticism was more cogent before 1936, when the traditional service was extensively revised, with the result that it became much more suitable for corporate use. In any case, the fact that Christian commitment has both individual and corporate aspects suggests that individual challenges can be felt and individual responses can be made within the context of public worship.

2. Covenant Services are unnecessary, because a once-for-all Covenant has been made in baptism. This argument raises an important theological point: nothing should be allowed to detract from the significance of the sacrament of baptism. But it is based upon a misunderstanding. Covenant Services do not create new Covenants; they are designed to be renewals of the Covenant which, indeed, we enter by baptism. If this is wrong, then so are a number of other practices—especially confirmation, which unquestionably fulfils the same sort of function, and the renewal of baptismal vows which some denominations undertake at regular intervals.

3. Covenant Services are unnecessary because the Church already possesses a sacrament—the Eucharist—which serves as a means whereby the baptismal Covenant may be regularly renewed. This objection rightly stresses that the Eucharist is an instrument of re-dedication. But the Eucharist has many other functions, and the renewal of the Covenant cannot be emphasized so strongly in the Eucharistic rite that those other functions are obscured. On certain occasions, it seems legitimate to place particular emphasis

THE COVENANT SERVICE

upon this important aspect of the Eucharist, just as particular doctrines are given special prominence week by week in the Christian Year even though the whole Gospel is celebrated in every act of worship. The Covenant Service should most certainly be associated with the Eucharist; it should indeed be a Eucharist 'with special intention'; but it is not, in the judgment of the present writer, rendered unnecessary simply because the Eucharist is itself an act of re-dedication.

We have spent some time in examining these background questions about the history, significance and appropriateness of Covenant Services because these services are very largely confined to Methodism. Every other rite in *The Methodist Service Book* has its parallel in the liturgies of almost every other denomination; this is not the case with THE COVENANT SERVICE. Having reached the conclusion that THE COVENANT SERVICE is a desirable form of worship, we may now turn to examine its contents.

As we have said, the revision of the service in 1936 was extensive, and although certain alterations have been made in the new rite, these are relatively minor changes. THE COVENANT SERVICE is held as part of a celebration of the Lord's Supper, and its structure is that of THE SUNDAY SERVICE, with the addition of the Covenant itself. Thus:

The Preparation
The Ministry of the Word
The Covenant
The Lord's Supper.

1. The Preparation

After a hymn, a responsive prayer of adoration is provided—a modernized version of a prayer from the 1936 service. A period of silence follows; then an act of confession—a modernized and abbreviated form of the 1936 confession—begins with responses, continues with silent confession, and concludes with a corporate reading of verses from Psalm 51. The minister reads a declaration of forgiveness. In 1936, an act of thanksgiving separated adoration and confession; this was necessary, in view of the inadequate provision of thanksgiving in the 1936 Eucharist, but it is now redundant: thanksgiving is reserved until later, when it will be fully expressed in the great prayer of THE SUNDAY SERVICE.

A special collect, followed by a hymn, brings the Preparation to a close.

2. The Ministry of the Word

The Old Testament lesson, the Epistle, the Gospel, the sermon and two hymns are the ingredients of this section of the service. The function of the Ministry of the Word, in this service as in others, is to make clear the significance of the act of response which is to follow, and indeed to invite those present to make the response. All three readings are highly appropriate.

3. The Covenant

Brief words of introduction, spoken by the minister, lead into this section. The nature of the Covenant is clearly stated: 'On the one side, God promises in this Covenant to give us new life in Christ. On the other

THE COVENANT SERVICE

side, we are pledged to live no more for ourselves but for him.' Then is sung the hymn, 'Come, let us use the grace divine', written by Charles Wesley specially for Covenant Services.

The minister now addresses the congregation, explaining what it means to stand within the Covenant, to serve Christ wholeheartedly regardless of the consequences. Then comes the most solemn moment of the service. The minister introduces the Covenant Prayer, in which the congregation joins. The prayer is a modernized version of the familiar and much-loved words of the 1936 service; apart from the change from 'Thou' to 'You' it is little altered. The Covenant Prayer is a fine piece of liturgical writing, which is quite rightly highly regarded by many Methodists. It is followed by the Lord's Prayer.

4. The Lord's Supper
The Lord's Supper begins, not from the Setting of the Table, as is the case with confirmation, but from the Peace. The Creed is omitted.

Questions for discussion
1. Compare THE COVENANT SERVICE with its equivalent of 1936. Discuss the ways in which the new service improves upon the old.

2. How significant is the idea of Covenant today?

3. Discuss the objections to the Covenant Service noted in this chapter.

4. Comment in detail on the Covenant Prayer (p. D10).

8 The Marriage Service

Unlike some other denominations, Methodism does not describe marriage as a sacrament, but it does recognize its important place as an ordinance of the Church. It is a feature of Christian worship that all the most special and significant moments of life can be catered for liturgically—birth, marriage and death are obvious examples. And, despite the increasing secularization of society, large numbers of men and women, many of whom are not practising Christians, continue to come to church to become man and wife. In part, no doubt, this is a matter of convention; there is still a widespread feeling that only marriages performed in church are 'real marriages', guaranteed to be blessed by God. When we add to this the attractiveness of a 'white wedding' with all the trimmings and an impressive ritual, and contrast this picture with the rather more stark marriage ceremony performed in Register Offices, it seems rather less surprising that many people who are not committed Christians choose to be married in church.

These reasons, of course, are inadequate; but this situation presents the Church with a fine opportunity to make pastoral contact with people at one of the most important moments of their lives. The value of this opportunity is emphasized in the General Directions, which state that the minister must 'ensure that the Christian understanding of marriage and its

THE MARRIAGE SERVICE

obligations is explained to the couple'. In one or more interviews, the minister can fulfil an important function as a disinterested yet concerned third party, helping the couple to understand the nature of the commitment into which they are entering and the solemn obligations that rest upon them.

Because marriage is a civil contract as well as a religious ceremony, certain parts of the service are prescribed by law. It is interesting and slightly amusing to note that, in this respect, the modern secular state has remained more conservative than the Church; the words required by law retain a number of archaic modes of expression, such as the pronoun 'thee'—said by the man to the woman and vice versa—which seem rather out of place in an otherwise modern form of service. For better or for worse, however, neither the Registrar-General nor the Houses of Parliament are subject to the authority of the Methodist Conference; and the legal words must remain in their traditional form until they are changed by Act of Parliament.

THE MARRIAGE SERVICE begins with the entry of the bride, who is met by her husband-to-be. The minister will, of course be present, and so will the registrar if the church is not registered for marriages solemnized by a minister acting as 'authorized person'. The law requires the presence of at least two witnesses. A hymn may be sung; then, while the congregation stands, the minister reads the Declaration of Purpose—a statement of the Christian understanding of marriage as 'the life-long union in body, mind and spirit, of one man and one woman'. The law then requires that the minister should ask whether anyone present knows of any reason why the couple may not lawfully be married. If anyone were to allege that an impediment to the marriage existed, the service would be interrupted, possibly deferred, until the complaint had been investigated. Fortunately, this happens extremely rarely. The man and the woman are now required to make a declaration that they themselves know of no lawful impediment to their marriage.

After the Collect for Purity, in the same version as is found in THE SUNDAY SERVICE, a short prayer of confession is said. Marriage is an immensely joyful occasion, so it is entirely right that this prayer should not be too heavily weighted with penitential phrases; words like 'love', 'enjoy', 'thankfulness', and 'praise' gear it to the tone of the occasion. Yet it is true that sin creates havoc in human relationships, even the most intimate; and confession for selfishness and ingratitude is not out of place in THE MARRIAGE SERVICE.

The Ministry of the Word may now follow. The minister reads what Jesus said about marriage (Matthew 19:4–6) and one or more passages from the epistles; an address may follow. As we have seen in previous chapters, this is liturgically the best place for the Ministry of the Word. The Word is first read and preached; then a specific act of response follows, such as baptism, or confirmation, or the renewal of the Covenant. But in the case of marriage, pastoral considerations may well override liturgical principles. Couples being married are almost invariably nervous, rightly conscious of the serious nature of what they are doing, and anxious to complete the rather frighten-

THE MARRIAGE SERVICE

ing business of making their vows. If the vows are held back until after the readings and an address, the sense of tension is made worse. Consequently, the whole of this section, or the address alone, may be deferred until later in the service, in which case the vows immediately follow the prayer of confession.

All stand, and the minister says a short prayer, asking that, through the power of the Holy Spirit, the couple may make and keep their vows. Then, in response to a question from the minister the man states that he will take the woman to be his lawful wedded wife; and the woman likewise answers that she will take the man to be her lawful wedded husband.

The next question and answer are optional. 'Who gives this woman to be married to this man?': 'I do.' The practice of 'giving away' the bride originated in the days when marriages were commonly arranged, often to form special contract relationships between families. It has long been recognized that women are not chattels, to be retained or given away by their families at will; but some couples feel that the 'giving away' implies such a belief. It is possible, however, to understand this ceremony as a symbol of the approval of the marriage on the part of the bride's family and the unity of the two families; and most couples do not object to it.

The minister now joins the right hand of the woman to that of the man, who then declares, in the presence of witnesses, that he takes the woman to be his lawful wedded wife. The first two lines of this vow are required by law; the remainder expresses more fully the Christian belief about marriage—that it is a commitment for life, in good circumstances and bad. The couple loose hands, and the woman then takes the right hand of the man in hers, making a similar promise.

Once again, the couple loose hands, and the ring(s) are laid on the minister's service book, usually by the best man. It is now quite common for the woman to give the man a ring, as well as receiving one from him, thus emphasizing the equal nature of the partnership. The minister says a prayer, asking God to bless the giving of the ring(s), that the couple may faithfully live together in love throughout their lives. Then the man receives the ring from the minister and places it on the fourth finger of the woman's left hand. (That, at least, is what the rubric says: liturgists obviously consider the thumb to be the first finger!) The woman may then give the man a ring. This section is concluded by a pledge made by the man and the woman together.

The vows and the exchange of ring(s) are complete, and a high point in the service is reached as the minister joins together the right hands of the couple, pronouncing them to be man and wife, and quoting the words of Jesus, 'Those whom God has joined together let no man put asunder'. It is good that these traditional words have been retained in preference to '... man must not separate', a revision favoured in some quarters,[1] which lacks the sonorous, impressive

---

[1] For example, the Order for Christian Marriage in Caryl Micklem (ed.), *Contemporary Prayers for Public Worship*, S.C.M. Press, 1967, p. 102.

THE MARRIAGE SERVICE

tones of the older translation. This is one of a few cases which can be noted in *The Methodist Service Book* where a traditional phrase or sentence is still to be preferred to a modern alternative.

The minister says a blessing for the couple; a pslam or hymn may be sung; and the Ministry of the Word—or the address only—if it was previously deferred, may come at this point. An act of intercession follows, preceded, if desired, by one or more of the additional prayers. The intercessions are primarily prayers for the newly-married couple, but one of them is for their families and friends. These intercessions are responsive, but if the congregation does not have copies of the service, they can be read by the minister alone. The Lord's Prayer follows.

Some couples wish their marriage to include a celebration of the Lord's Supper, and the most satisfactory part of THE SUNDAY SERVICE from which to begin would be the Setting of the Table. It is obvious that, for practising Christians, the linking of marriage with the Eucharist is most appropriate; it may be thought, however, that since the Eucharist is a sacrament of the whole Christian community, all communicant members present should be able to receive the elements, as well as the couple and the minister. This would probably take too long; in any case, it would segregate the practising Christians from the others present; for reasons such as these, some couples prefer not to proceed to the Lord's Supper.

If the Eucharist does not follow, a fine prayer of thanksgiving is said, the congregation joining in the *Sanctus*, and the minister says the Grace or some other blessing. This brings the service proper to a close: the couple and the minister now usually retire to the vestry for the signing of the registers.

The experimental form of marriage service which preceded *The Methodist Service Book* won wide acceptance because of its simplicity, directness, and intrinsic beauty. In this, its final form, it is much to be preferred to the rather more wordy and archaic service of 1936.

Service for the Blessing of a Marriage Previously Solemnized

It sometimes happens that a couple, previously married in a Register Office, wish to have a religious service in church. The minister may either read THE MARRIAGE SERVICE—without repeating those vows which have already been made—or use a special form of service. The latter course is the better, because the service is designed for the purpose, though its basic structure is that of THE MARRIAGE SERVICE, and its compilers have clearly tried to reproduce as much of that service as possible.

An amended form of the Declaration of Purpose is read, followed by the Collect for Purity and the prayer of confession. Then comes the Ministry of the Word —without provision for its deferment—with the same readings as in THE MARRIAGE SERVICE, and an address. The vows are altered to take into account the fact that the couple have already taken each other as husband and wife; the promises they now make embody the Christian principles of love, honour and fidelity.

THE MARRIAGE SERVICE

The giving of the ring(s) has already taken place, but the service includes prayer over the ring(s), with the prayer of blessing suitably altered. The couple's subsequent declaration acknowledges that God has bound them together in Christian marriage for the duration of their lives. The remainder of the service is identical to THE MARRIAGE SERVICE.

Both these new services are excellent. Here is liturgy that is lively and joyful, lucid and, in the best sense, up to date, entirely suitable for the occasions when these services will be used.

Questions for discussion

1. Should marriage in church be restricted to practising Christians?

2. Discuss the meaning of Christian marriage, with particular reference to the Declaration of Purpose.

3. Discuss your reactions to the language of this new service.

4. Discuss the circumstances in which the SERVICE FOR THE BLESSING OF A MARRIAGE PREVIOUSLY SOLEMNIZED might be required, and comment on its appropriateness.

9 The Burial or Cremation of the Dead

We have already observed the claim of Christian worship to be able to meet people at all the most significant stages in their lives—from the cradle to the grave. The Christian religion centres on a death and resurrection; it is, therefore, able to offer comfort and hope to those who mourn. The provision of a liturgical rite to mark a human death is a valued part of the service which the Church offers to the community, not merely to those who are practising Christians.

Although the basic structure and the content of the 1936 service were sound, the language of the prayers and the Bible readings was archaic. The new service resembles its predecessor in many ways, the biggest change being in language. Some of the prayers and Scripture readings are modernized versions of texts which appeared in 1936. The general structure is similar, though its components are more clearly distinguished, and more provision is made for variation. The note of Christian confidence in the presence of death is perhaps more clearly sounded in the new service than it was in 1936.

THE BURIAL OR CREMATION OF THE DEAD has the following structure:

> The Entry (not, in fact, thus designated in *The Methodist Service Book*)
> The Ministry of the Word

THE BURIAL OR CREMATION OF THE DEAD

Thanksgiving
Commendation
Committal.

1. The Entry

Sometimes, the greater part of the service takes place in church or in a cemetery chapel, the Committal being reserved for use at the graveside or at the crematorium. On other occasions, the whole service is read at the crematorium. Wherever the service begins, the minister meets the body and goes before it, reading one or more of a selection of Scripture sentences. These sentences are words of hope and faith. Then, when those who have followed the body have reached their places, a hymn may be sung and one of three prayers from the text or one of the first three additional prayers may be said.

2. The Ministry of the Word

The introduction to this section, spoken by the minister, is a powerful and succinct statement of the Christian hope which sustains us in the presence of death. As well as introducing the readings which follow, these words set the tone of the whole service.

Psalm 130, which may be followed by either Psalm 23 or verses from Psalm 103, or both, introduces the readings; then, one or more passages from the New Testament should be read: a considerable degree of choice is possible. This is good: at some funerals, for example in the case of a person who has been a faithful and devoted Christian, certain readings will be highly appropriate which would be out of place in different circumstances. Sufficient readings are recommended to make it possible for the most suitable to be used.

A sermon may be preached. It is desirable that some sort of address, however brief, should follow the readings, unless there are exceptional circumstances which make this difficult. When appropriate, something should be said about the person who is being buried or cremated; there should also be reference to the Christian Gospel of life and hope and to the promise of consolation to those who mourn. It is sometimes suitable for the congregation to say the Apostles' Creed after the sermon, as a summary of the Christian faith; the parts of the Creed which refer to death and resurrection are particularly appropriate.

3. Thanksgiving

Thanksgiving is a vital ingredient of worship; indeed, the principal act of Christian worship—the Eucharist—is primarily concerned with thanksgiving. It is one of the glories of Christianity that what seems to be a deeply sad occasion can be accompanied by thanksgiving; that there can be joy in the midst of sorrow, and peace at a time of distress. As the introduction to the Ministry of the Word says, 'in the presence of death, Christians have sure ground for hope and confidence, and even for joy'. Many readers will have had experience of attending the funeral of a member of a deeply committed Christian family at which there has been a truly joyous atmosphere, hope and thankfulness. Such experiences are to be treasured; they are comparatively rare. Not everyone finds it easy to

THE BURIAL OR CREMATION OF THE DEAD

respond to death in this way. But the Gospel remains the same; and though they may find this truth difficult to grasp, Christians who mourn the loss of loved ones have deep grounds for thanksgiving.

The first prayer in this section is a joyous thanksgiving for the redeeming work of Christ, especially through his death and resurrection, and for the hope of everlasting life. This excellent prayer had no direct equivalent in the 1936 service: its introduction is one of the most welcome features of the new rite. It is a most fitting response to the Ministry of the Word which precedes it.

The second prayer is a thanksgiving for God's 'departed servants'—for their lives, for the congregation's memories of them, and for their release from 'the tribulations of this world'.

4. Commendation

A solemn moment is reached, as the congregation stands and the minister says the words of commendation, confidently commending the dead person, by name, to the care of God. This is followed by the Lord's Prayer, and unless the whole service is taking place in a crematorium chapel, the words of Hebrew 13:20 f bring this section of the service to a close. The body is now transported to the cemetery or crematorium, and once again the minister, preceding the body, may read one or more Scripture sentences. The body is laid in the earth or on the catafalque.

5. Committal

The words of committal are said by the minister, while

the congregation stands. The first form of committal is normally used; the second and shorter version is intended to be used when the wording of the first form is thought inappropriate. The minister says the traditional words of Revelation 14:13. A prayer follows, that those present may, like the one who has died, finally come into the joy of the Kingdom; and a number of other prayers are available for use after this. Although some people have theological difficulties about praying for the dead others find the practice helpful. Optional prayers for the dead are, therefore, included in this service.

The Burial or Cremation of a Child
However strong our faith may be, the death of a loved one is naturally accompanied by sorrow; but there is something specially heart-rending about the death of a child, whose life has barely started and whose promise is unfulfilled. In 1936, a special service was supplied for the funeral of a child; but, as a matter of principle, the compilers of the new service have thought it best to provide only one basic form of service. Nevertheless, they have found it necessary to suggest certain changes in the service when a child is to be buried or cremated.

It is taken for granted that the service needs to be brief, and that the permitted variations should be adapted at the minister's discretion. It is suggested that Psalm 23 should be said instead of or in addition to Psalm 130, and that John 14:1–6, 27, a passage full of re-assurance for those who mourn, should be read. The use of Mark 10:13–16 is also

THE BURIAL OR CREMATION OF THE DEAD

strongly commended: this is one of the Gospel readings in THE BAPTISM OF INFANTS, and this association adds to its real appropriateness in the context of the funeral of a child.

A special form of committal is also supplied, together with prayers for use instead of or in addition to the post-committal prayers provided in the main service. The judicious use of these variants can lead to a service which is both brief and appropriate.

The fact of death is inescapable. We may try not to think about it, much less discuss it; but, in the end, we must all die. People differ in their attitudes to their own deaths: some do not consider the matter; others fear death; yet others, as long lives draw to a close, welcome the prospect of death. Similarly, close relations and friends react in different ways when a loved one dies: there are those who are overwhelmed with grief, those who display a lively and even joyful faith, and the majority whose reaction lies somewhere between those extremes.

Ministers and lay visitors try, when circumstances allow, to care for the dying and to comfort the bereaved. It is not the easiest of tasks, but it is an important part of our service. And we are strengthened to offer help and comfort in these ways by the good news which we are able to proclaim—good news about life which transcends death, good news about the infinite love and mercy of God from which nothing in all creation can separate us. It is one of the glories of our religion that it refuses to allow death the last word: 'O death, where is thy victory? ...

Thanks be to God, who gives us the victory through our Lord Jesus Christ.'

But most people, when a relation or a close friend dies, do not find that such hope and confidence come to them easily. Feelings of grief and loss—even, sometimes, of remorse or anger—are stronger. So the Christian friend must be patient and sympathetic, understanding the strength of these emotions and helping the bereaved to come to terms with their feelings and to stumble through them to faith and hope. A funeral service, as well as providing fitting liturgy to mark the end (on earth) of a human life, needs to play a part in the comforting of those who mourn. For this purpose THE BURIAL OR CREMATION OF THE DEAD is admirably suitable; and this is not the least of its merits.

Questions for discussion
1. 'For Christians, death is the supreme festival.' Do you agree? Does the new burial service reflect this opinion?

2. What improvements have been made in the new funeral service, as compared with that of 1936?

3. Discuss what parts of the service you would use—if the decision were yours—for the funeral of a person who was not a practising Christian.

4. How can the Church help the bereaved?

10 The Ordinaton of Ministers

Every year, one evening in early July, three or four large churches are packed to the doors. At each, admission is by ticket only, a rare experience in itself for most Methodists. The crowds gather to witness one of the most impressive of our occasional services, the ordination of ministers.

Becoming a minister of the Word and the Sacraments is a process which takes several years, and one or two long-overdue reforms which are about to be introduced in the procedure will not greatly alter that.

The traditional and present procedure is that a period of testing and training precedes entry into theological college, where courses take up to four years. Then students become probationer ministers and spend a couple of years in the circuits of Methodism, while their academic training continues and their pastoral experience widens. At the end of this period, if their progress is satisfactory, they are presented for ordination.

Earlier in the day on which they are to be ordained, the ordinands are 'received into full connexion' by a standing vote of the Methodist Conference which is then in session. The relationship between ordination and reception into full connexion is roughly equivalent to that between confirmation and reception into full membership: Methodism originated as a Society within the Church, and as such it receives new members and new ministers; as a Church it confirms and ordains.

But what is ordination, and how is an ordained minister different from a probationer or a layman? A good deal of ink has been used in trying to answer questions such as these, especially in recent years when there has been much emphasis upon the role of the layman and the varied 'ministries' that can be exercised by people both ordained and lay. Interest in the theology of 'laymanship' has inevitably provoked examination of what it means to be an ordained minister.

The Methodist doctrine of the ordained ministry is different from the Anglican, Roman Catholic, and Orthodox doctrine of the priesthood. 'The Methodist Church holds the doctrine of the priesthood of all believers and consequently believes that no priesthood exists which belongs exclusively to a particular order or class of men. . .'[1] In the New Testament, the whole Church is described as priestly: 'you are . . . a royal priesthood'.[2] The whole people of God shares the priestly calling. But 'in the exercise of (the Church's) corporate life and worship special qualifications for the discharge of special duties are required and thus the principle of representative selection is recognised';[3] within the Body, some individuals are called to have 'a principal and directing part' as 'Stewards in the household of God and Shepherds of the His flock'.[4]

---

[1] *Deed of Union*, clause 30.
[2] I Peter 2:9.
[3] *Deed of Union*, clause 30.
[4] Ibid.

THE ORDINATION OF MINISTERS

Some of the functions fulfilled by ordained ministers are shared with others—for instance, visiting the sick, preaching, and administration. Others, notably that of presiding at the Eucharist, are reserved for ordained ministers. Within the Church, ministers are representative persons: '... in their office the calling of the whole Church is focused and represented ... in this sense they are the sign of the presence and ministry of Christ in the Church, and through the Church to the world.'[5]

It is generally understood that becoming a minister depends upon the call of God. The ministry is not a profession which anyone who has the necessary academic qualifications can enter if he finds it attractive: it is literally a vocation, and the Church would not consider for its ministry a candidate who could not testify to a sense of call, to an inner compulsion to offer himself for this work. That is the first requirement. But it is not enough; a man may be mistaken in sensing a call. So the Church must test the call through the procedures of candidature, ministerial training and probation. The individual's sense of vocation is thus 'recognized and confirmed by the corporate judgment of the Church'.[6]

With all this in mind, we turn to the new service, THE ORDINATION OF MINISTERS. It is interesting to note that this rite is unique among the other new services in that no experimental form preceded it during the 1960s. An ordination service was, however, included

[5] *Report on Ordination*, adopted by the Methodist Conference of 1974, p. 7.
[6] Ibid., p. 6.

in the Anglican-Methodist Unity Scheme, and although this was never used, it has clearly influenced the compilers of THE ORDINATION OF MINISTERS.

The new service is divided thus:

The Ministry of the Word
The Presentation
The Examination
The Ordination
The Lord's Supper.

1. The Ministry of the Word

A hymn and a special collect—which may be preceded or followed by the Collect of the Day—are followed by three Bible readings and a sermon. The Nicene Creed is then recited.

This section of the service clearly resembles its equivalent in other rites. Once again, the lessons and the sermon represent the Word of God which evokes a response from us—whether that is expressed in the Lord's Supper, or Baptism, or Confirmation, or the renewal of the Covenant, or in some other way. In ordination also, the order is highly appropriate. A man becomes a minister in response to God's call; it is therefore right that the ordination service should begin with the reading and exposition of part of God's Word.

2. The Preparation

The service is conducted by the President and Secretary of the Conference, or their representatives. After the Ministry of the Word, the Secretary presents to

THE ORDINATION OF MINISTERS

the President those who are to be ordained 'Presbyters'. This unfamiliar word calls for explanation. In New Testament times, there were apparently two orders of ministry: there were *deacons*, whose main function was to care for the needy, and *presbyters* or *bishops*, who preached, administered the sacraments, and acted as 'overseers'. At first, there was no distinction between presbyters and bishops; but as time passed, some churches came to have a three-fold ministry of deacons, presbyters (sometimes called priests) and bishops. Methodism has deaconesses but no male deacons; and the relationship between the diaconate (the order of deacons) and the presbyterate (the ordained ministry of Word and Sacraments) is not entirely clear. Although most of us have no strong theological objection to the distinction between presbysters and bishops, it has been our practice to have only one order of ministry. Although the word 'presbyter' has not been widely used in Methodism, it was employed in the Draft Ordinal (an ordinal is an ordination service) which formed part of the Anglican-Methodist Unity Scheme. Since the Church of England has a three-fold ministry, Methodist ministers would be regarded as members of the second order, the presbyterate, if the two churches were to unite.

The Presentation is a significant moment in the service. Many men and women have recognized, in Circuit Meetings, Synods, examination committees, and the Conference itself, that the candidates are called by God. They are represented by the Secretary, who reads out the candidates' names, and by the congregation, which gives the final assent to the ordination of the candidates in response to a question asked by the President. The President, the Secretary, and the congregation act not only on their own behalf, but as representatives of the whole Church.

3. The Examination
Although the candidates have been tested in various ways during the years that have led up to this moment, 'it has generally been thought desirable that they should pledge themselves publicly to certain things before being actually ordained'.[7] Thus certain questions are asked of them. The whole Church has spoken; now the individual candidates express their personal commitment as they affirm their sense of call, their acceptance of the Scriptures and Christian doctrine and the discipline of the Church, and their resolution to pray and study. There are fewer questions than there were in the 1936 service, but nothing essential has been omitted.

4. The Ordination
As the moment of ordination approaches, the President bids the congregation pray for those who are to be ordained. Then the President sums up the congregation's silent prayers; and a translation of the ancient Latin hymn, *Veni Creator Spiritus*, which has long been associated with ordination rites, is sung. (In the Draft Ordinal, this part of the service is called the Supplication.)

[7] *Anglican-Methodist Unity*, 'Part 1, The Ordinal', p. 6.

THE ORDINATION OF MINISTERS

In the Early Church, men were ordained by prayer accompanied by the laying on of hands. If more than one candidate is to be ordained and the prayer is fairly long, this ancient practice raises a practical difficulty: a lengthy prayer cannot be repeated several times, nor can the same hands be laid on several heads simultaneously. Various modifications of the ancient practice have therefore been adopted. In the 1936 service, for example, the President lays his hands upon the head of each ordinand after the ordination prayer, saying further words to each ordinand as he does so. This is not a good solution to the problem, for the words that accompany the action draw attention away from the prayer. The recommendation of the Draft Ordinal has been accepted in THE ORDINATION OF MINISTERS: the practice of the Church of South India has been adopted.

This practice is as follows. The ordination prayer is in three parts: the first is a thanksgiving; the second is a petition for the bestowal of the Spirit, and this is repeated for each ordinand, accompanied by the laying on of hands; the third is a prayer that the new ministers may faithfully fulfil their calling. By repeating the central petition as many times as is necessary, the difficulties of combining prayer and action are satisfactorily overcome.

The ordination prayer is followed by the Lord's Prayer and the traditional ceremony of giving a Bible to each new minister. The President then declares that those who have been ordained have authority to preach the Word and administer the Sacraments, and exhorts them to be good and faithful ministers.

5. The Lord's Supper
The Peace is exchanged between the President and the congregation, and THE SUNDAY SERVICE is followed from the Setting of the Table. A special post-communion prayer is supplied.

Almost every minister ordained according to the rite of 1936 has poignant memories of his ordination, a most significant moment in his life. Yet that service, moving though it was, sorely needed revision. Its language was archaic; its length innordinate; some of its contents, especially the promises, were no longer suitable. THE ORDINATION OF MINISTERS clearly expresses the significance of what takes place in ordination, in terms appropriate to the modern world.

This chapter concludes our brief examination of *The Methodist Service Book*. The Methodist people owe a great debt to the liturgical scholars who have provided them with these excellent new forms of worship. It is to be hoped that, despite other financial pressures, every local church will consider the purchase of *The Methodist Service Book* to be a high priority; that ministers and local preachers will make good use of the material that it provides; that congregations will study the new services and seek to use them effectively; and that, in consequence, *The Methodist Service Book* will lead to the enrichment of worship and the deepening of spiritual life throughout the Methodist Church.

Questions for discussion
1. 'We're all ministers!' If that is true, what does ordination signify?

THE ORDINATION OF MINISTERS

2. Compare the questions on p. G9 with those asked in the 1936 service. Discuss the reasons that might have led the compilers of the new service to omit those they have removed and to revise those they have retained.

3. If possible, discuss with a minister what significance his ordination has had for him.

4. Discuss the extent to which the following constitute life-long commitments: baptism, confirmation, marriage, ordination.

Addendum

The following services have been authorized by the Methodist Conference and thus have the same authority as the contents of *The Methodist Service Book*, although they are not included in it.

RECOGNITION AND COMMISSIONING SERVICES
(The Recognition and Commissioning of Local Preachers; the Recognition and Commissioning of Class Leaders; the Recognition and Commissioning of Workers with Children and Young People.)
THE WELCOME OF A MINISTER
THANKSGIVING OF PARENTS FOR THE BIRTH OF A CHILD

www.ingramcontent.com/pod-product-compliance
Lightning Source LLC
Chambersburg PA
CBHW072010090426
42734CB00033B/2418